in your own skin

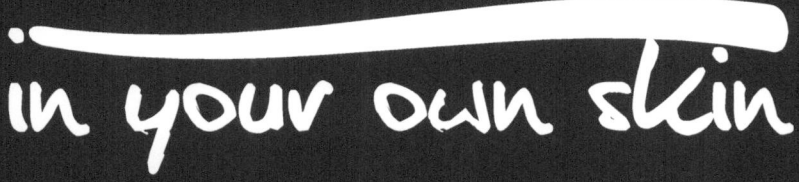

in your own skin

Katheryn Trenshaw

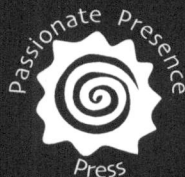

Passionate Presence Center for Creative Expression
www.inyourownskin.org

Praise for *In Your Own Skin:*

"In Your Own Skin is an inspiring attempt to awaken our deep need for community. The project creates a sort of "song line" of humanity's vulnerability and heartfelt yearning for connection. In today's world, a welcome application of creative spirit."

- Helena Norberg-Hodge, director of the *International Society for Ecology and Culture* (ISEC), film producer of *The Economics of Happiness*

"In Your Own Skin is a beautiful depiction of our shared humanity."

- Juliet Russell, singer and vocal coach on BBC1's *The Voice UK*

"In Your Own Skin celebrates and reveals not just a biodiversity of people but the diversity within each person. Because of the artist's challenging invitation to her subjects, the project also illuminates and plays with the fascinating gap between the way we see ourselves and the way we imagine we're seen. We glimpse the elusive, fluctuating space between the image and the self-image."

- Matt Harvey, author *The Hole in the Sum of My Parts*

"In Your Own Skin is a moving innovative project that has the potential to make Katheryn Trenshaw a household name. Its genius lies in the absolute vulnerability and beauty of this photographic magnum opus."

- Malcolm Stern, psychotherapist, TV presenter, & author of *The Courage to Love*

"The *In Your Own Skin* Project is a fascinating concept, beautifully realized. What are the secrets we carry deep beneath the surface, and what would it be like to wear them on our skin?"

- Starhawk, author and filmmaker, *The Fifth Sacred Thing*

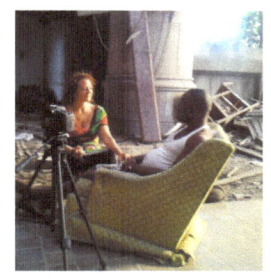

introduction

Through a face, a look or body language we believe we can tell all sorts of things about another person. It is almost second nature to us to project all kinds of ideas about who people are and what they are about; 'mother', 'rich', 'attractive', 'miserable,' 'young and excitable', 'works with his hands' and so on. We also tend to presume a deeper knowledge: socio-economic level, education, familial background and sexual orientation as if we can divine much from a brief glimpse. Although these speculations may contain some truth, these habitual assumptions are not necessarily held consciously.

Everyone has a story. Many people think they can 'read' others' stories in their appearance. However, as Antoine de Saint-Exupéry said, "Life always bursts the boundaries of formulas." *In Your Own Skin* celebrates this concept.

In my practice as an artist, therapist, consultant and teacher for over thirty years, I have consistently explored human expression and wellbeing. Ultimately I am interested in the essential qualities of what makes human beings happy, or unhappy. As my research developed, I realized that the answer is directly related to how we choose to show ourselves to the world. And what's even more interesting is what we choose to leave concealed or hidden. It is a popular myth that vulnerability equals weakness. We are often swayed into believing it is easier to experience 'belonging' if we appear to 'fit in' and 'seem ok'.

As an insatiably curious cultural creative, with extensive training in Psychology and embodied consciousness, I am fascinated by the idea of 'revealing the concealed'. My life's work has taught me again and again that it is this deep place where real intimacy and vulnerability lie. As the worthiness and shame research of Brené Brown, the author of *The Gifts of Imperfection* shows, 'Vulnerability is our most accurate measurement of courage.' This edgy place is often where we fear visiting the most, and is paradoxically the gateway to innovation, creativity and vitality. It is also the doorway to connection and happiness.

When we give ourselves permission to speak the unspeakable, we unwrap the layers like removing thick ivy tightly wound around a tree. These layers conceal but do not eliminate the tree, i.e. our true nature. The tree is still whole and already there. And when we stop fiercely defending our stories, and peel back the contortions, we are simply free to express the beauty of who we really are.

Many ingredients spiraled together to spark the idea for this project. Some of them include, in no particular order: my fascination with the invisible within the visible through art; the fact that my mother read quantum physics for leisure when I was a young child before it was cool or even readily available information; the neurobiological research that shows how we are hardwired to connect; eight years of penmanship in Catholic grade school; a gift for body painting; and my own lifelong involvement with travel, the arts, and somatic practices. This seemingly disparate bunch of influences conspired together in my creative heart and said, "Aha! Here's what you will be focusing on for the next period of your life." Thus the *In Your Own Skin* project was born.

I knew as soon as I prepared to do my first portrait, camera in hand and questions at the ready, that the *In Your Own Skin* project was going to be a book, a film and an exhibit. The idea was so simple: I asked each subject to come up with a word or phrase that would express who they really are, daring them to answer the provocative question: **What is true of you that is not obvious to strangers?** The next step was then to paint the response somewhere on their body, making it skin-deep, exposing the naked truth for 'all' to see. As you might imagine the process was incredibly personal to each subject, sometimes funny, and often very moving. I felt deeply privileged to witness the wit, humor and raw beauty many were willing to share.

Of course each portrait invites the viewer to inquire into their own heart with these same kinds of questions. We are curious about the photos in the same way we are curious about what is revealed when we look into a mirror. Our story is all of these stories. Like the painter Mark Rothko speaks of his chapel paintings in Houston, "Art is just a mirror. You are just looking at yourself."

I didn't anticipate quite how potent the process would be for the individual involved either. As I progressed with the portraits, I saw how, for the subjects, this was akin to a rite of passage and a laying down of something old and ripe. And as I continued to photograph people (friends, acquaintances and strangers) with whom I explored this inquiry, more and more people expressed interest in having their portrait taken. For the most part people have jumped at the chance to have their portraits done. Once I had photographed friends, I progressed to people I didn't know. Perhaps they looked interesting or seemed like they might have an intriguing story. Sometimes I overheard people talking and approached them. I once met a family in Mexico and photographed the son. Pretty soon I had over 100 photographic portraits of people of all ages from around the globe from USA to UK, Mexico to Morocco, Sweden to Switzerland.

There is a simple message behind each portrait. It says 'Look, we are all human and we all carry invisible stories, powerful and vulnerable. It's time for me to take courage and share the parts of me that I normally keep hidden. I am learning about how to peel back to the truth and be comfortable in my own skin, and you can too.' For some people it takes a while to get to the answer to the question, "What is true of you but not obvious to strangers?" I then asked the question in different ways: "What are your paradoxes?" or "What lives in the liminal space where the two worlds touch?" or "What would people in your day-to-day world never guess just from looking at you?" And of course my presence makes a difference. I'm a non-judgmental witness. This simple yet powerful way of being with another enables people to relax. Because of my professional training and my life experience I'm able to put people at ease and am not easily shocked. I never know what I'm going to get. It's a journey we take together. As one of the subjects said, "The main art is the conversation."

In Your Own Skin celebrates the intimate essence of humanity.

Everyone has a powerful story. What is your story?

What word would *you* choose?

for my son, Orion

photographs

"To be human
is to become visible
while carrying
what is hidden
as a gift to others."

- David Whyte, from *What to Remember When Waking*

incapacitating depression

name: Moa
age: 50
born: Sweden

Moa's story is so memorable. She seems like an obvious place to begin. I was having lunch in the café of the British Museum in London (one of my favorite museums) waiting for a young man for a photo shoot for the project. I got talking to a cheery middle-aged Swedish woman. The café was packed so we shared a small table. She asked what I was doing, so I told her about the *In Your Own Skin* project. She was a total stranger but an hour later she was standing on the front steps of the museum, 'clinically depressed for 15 years' written onto her décolletage having her portrait taken in the middle of hoards of tourists who had no doubt come to see quite a different exhibition.

In the short time we spent together she told me that this was the first time she had been away from her husband and it felt like a big adventure to be in London on her own. I never would have guessed that this woman had suffered with severe depression, let alone for so long. I could see that just having told someone her painful story was such a relief for her.

Unbeknownst to her, while she had been at the museum, her husband had a stroke at home in Sweden. She wrote to me weeks later to tell me this. The tone of her letter was keen to convey how important our chance encounter had been to her. She explained how the process of having her portrait taken had somehow empowered her, and provided the ground for a newfound sense of strength and courage she had needed in order to face this recent crisis. She went on to describe the sensation of 'wholeness' she was experiencing as a result, and couldn't thank me enough for allowing her to give voice to what had been so secreted away.

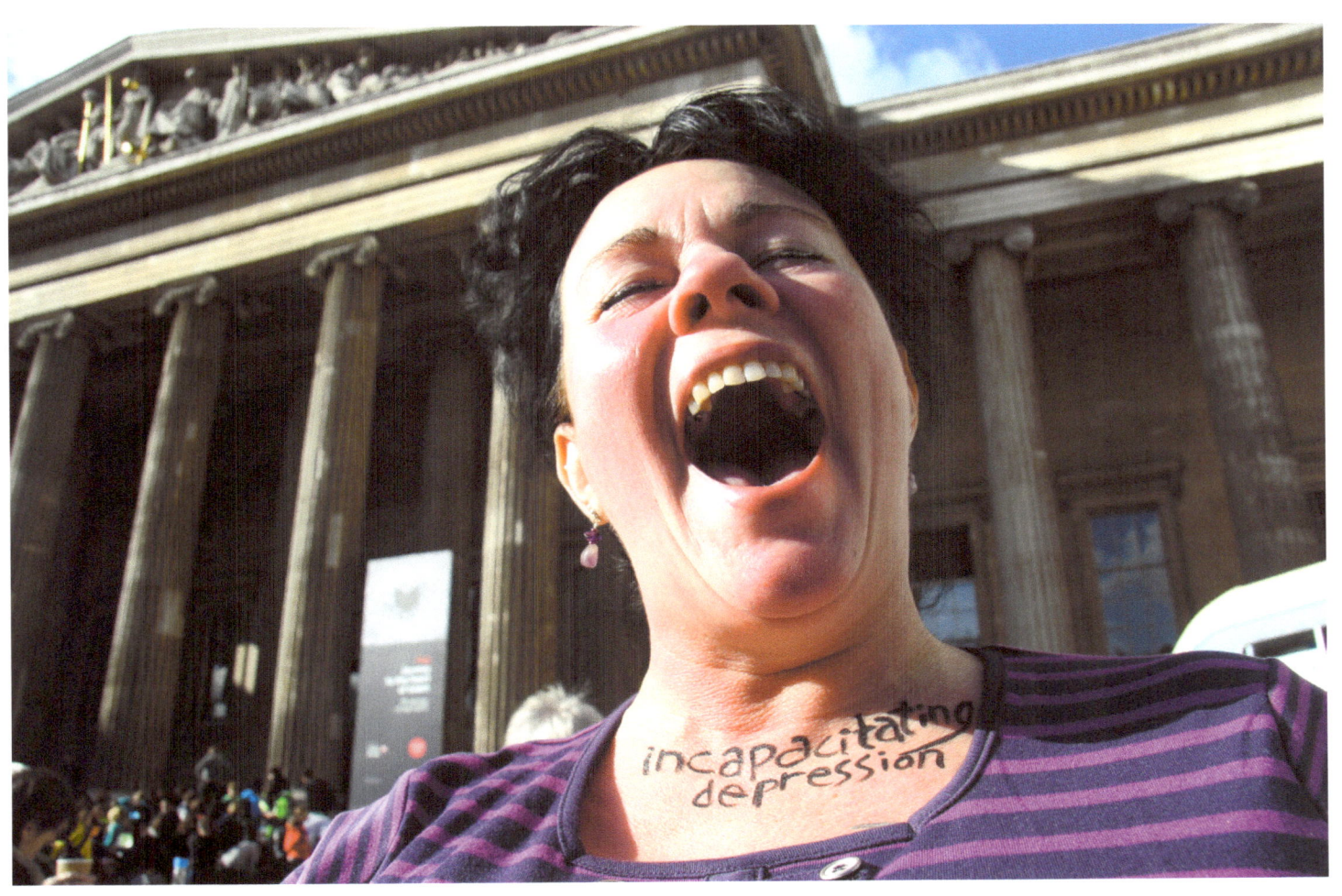

mother

name: Yusra
age: 26
born: United Arab Emirites

Yusra is charming and articulate. When we meet, I am drawn to her and also a bit nervous and unsure if she will talk to me. I've just seen her on stage at a conference. She is a performance poet and an actress. I find her very beautiful, but any hesitation I hold melts immediately on starting a conversation with her.

She is young. I had guessed in her late teens. As it turns out, she's 26. That is partly why she chose to write mother. People think she's just a child herself, but she has two children already. They are four years and twenty months. They have changed everything for her and turned her world inside out. "But everything is inside out anyway!" she proclaims. "The earth, the person you came from, everything turns inside out to make way. And you are all going to be with the mother eventually. Inside out." She proudly shows me her belly streaked generously with stretch marks. She calls them her battle scars. "Having a child does something for you and more. We never hear about how much

children teach their parents and are powerful mirrors. Who's raising who? I make a child. But the child makes me a woman." She loves being a mother.

In her family's Islamic tradition, it is understood that heaven lies at the feet of the mother. "Your mother can call you out of prayer, and you must listen to the mother three times before the father." Her mom was a Somali nomad and her dad was a Muslim from Yemen. They moved to the United Arab Emirates and eventually to Manchester in the United Kingdom. She speaks proudly of the things that made her: Family made me. Manchester made me. Somalia made me.

She rounded out our conversation nicely by saying, "Don't be scared to be ugly and true." I couldn't agree more. And we were both uplifted by a shared appreciation and embrace of the paradox in this statement.

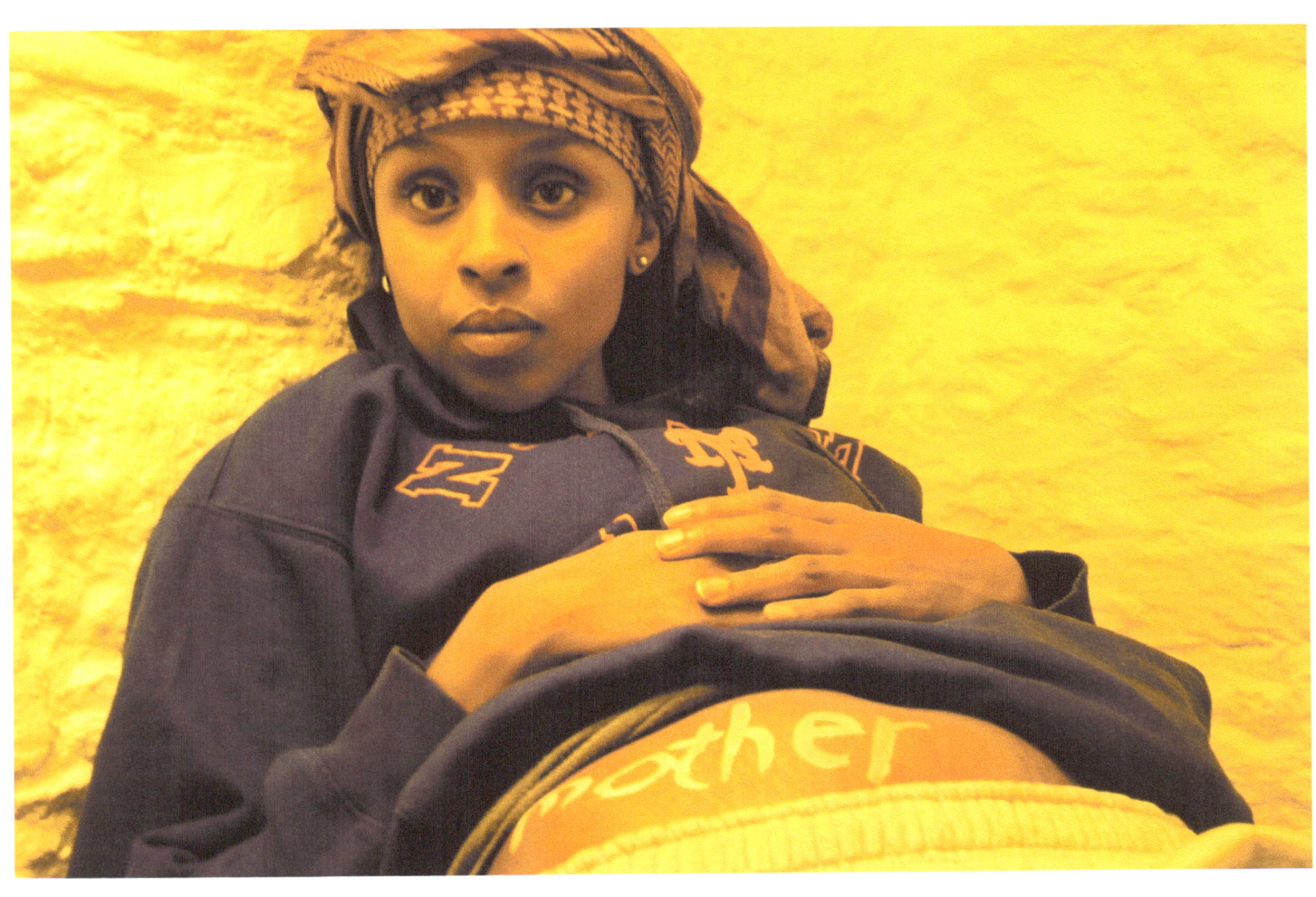

Raped

name: Anonymous
age: 30
born: anonymous

"Because I am young and relatively healthy and some would say even good looking, they would never guess that I had been raped. I wanted to challenge the stereotype. We look normal...all of us who have survived this. We ARE normal, beautiful, powerful, vibrant... only we have been through this particular experience.

Having said that, at first I really wanted to be fully seen as I am in this portrait and be a stand for all of us, but then I realized that I could not go to work on Monday and have to deal with all the consequences. It is still too taboo. That is sad, but that is also just the way it is. And I am happy and well and loved and supported in my life. And I want to be a stand against rape and for freedom."

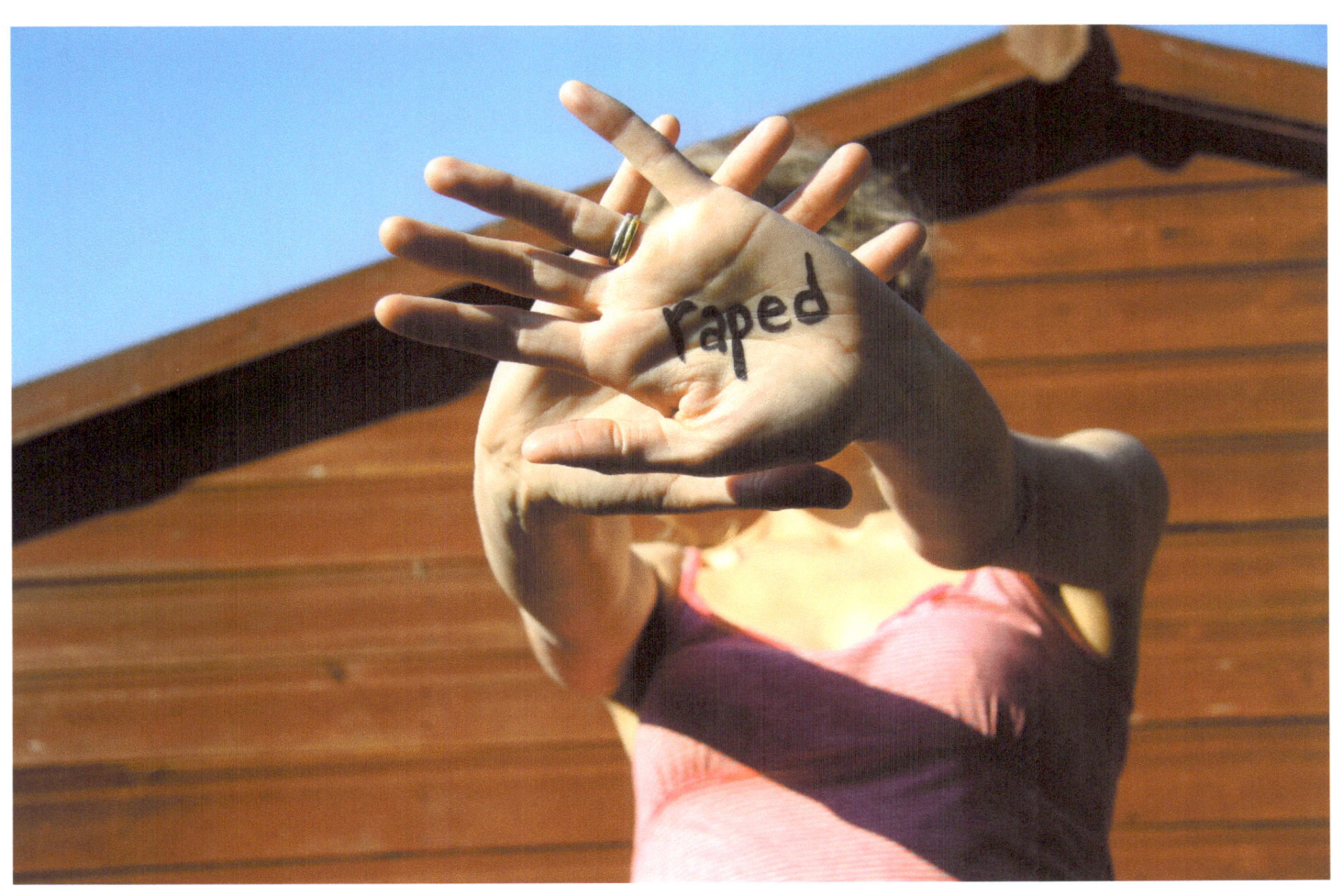

odd sock wearer

name: Solomon
age: 11
born: England

"I'm a bit unique…some people call me eccentric.
But I am just creative and an original. And, for some
reason, I decided one day not to be too normal and
started always wearing odd socks. Most people don't
notice, but it's kind of my "thing". I like to be different
and a bit mad. Some people say I am a genius. I like
that."

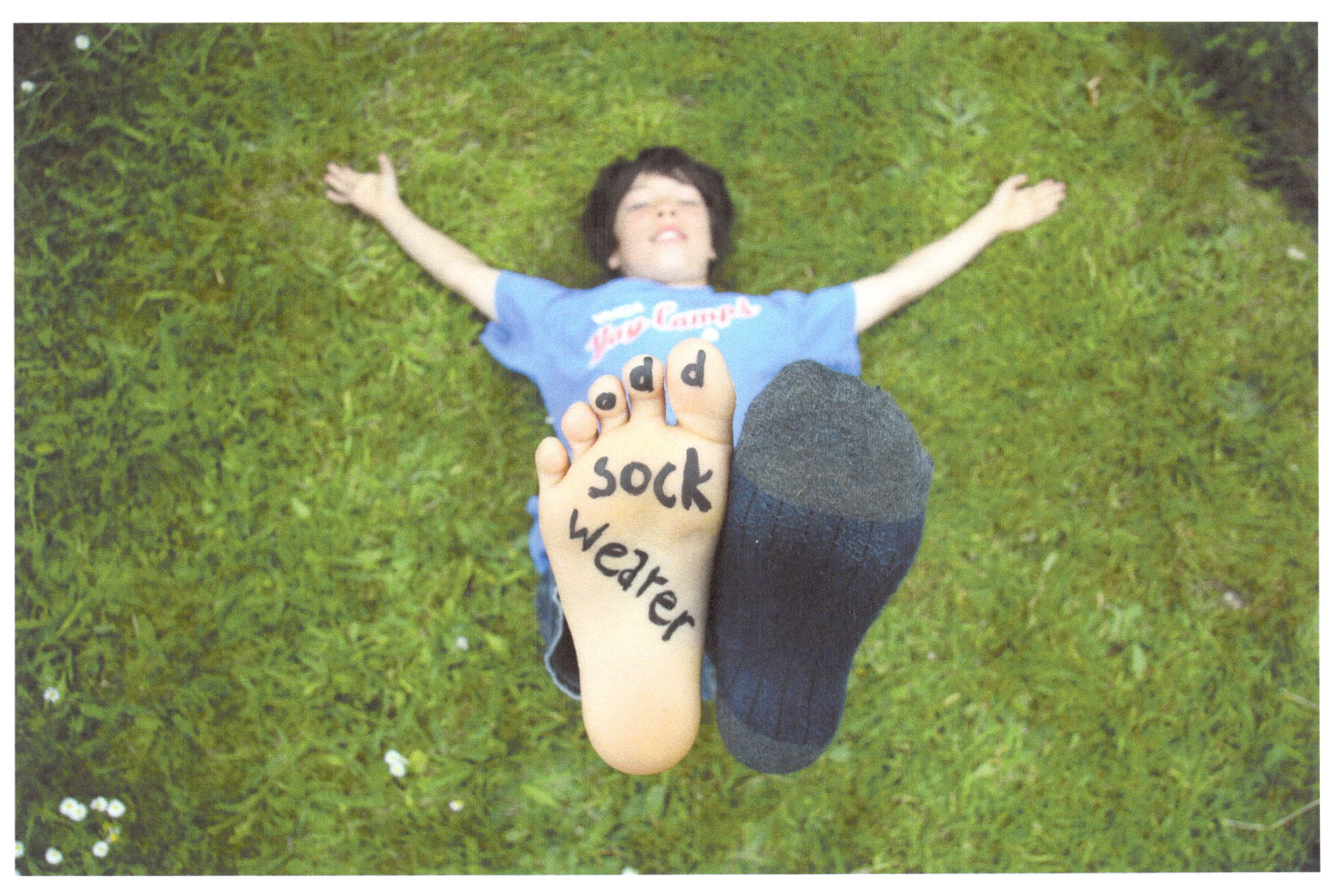

gift
name: Paradox
age: 45
born: England

"I used to be a very successful and ambitious marketing and media professional. At 33 years old, I got disillusioned with this work and how it wasn't contributing enough to the planet. One day I was called to just give it all up in quite an extreme way and I became homeless. It was then, living in Battersea Park in London, that my alter ego was born and I became Paradox, the performance poet. This led me to a great number of rich counterculture collaborations.

One of these happened in 2008 where I went traveling in Mexico as a part of a 'rainbow cowboy horse caravan circus', as you do. We took the horses to the river one day and there were local kids there climbing and jumping in off of a cliff. They usually did this when 30 gringos rode into town. They were simply showing off. I couldn't resist and they made it look so easy. I stood just where they were jumping in. And just where I jumped there was a rock sticking out of the river bed which I hit. I got gangrene and nearly died.

My friends became absolute angels. They campaigned, without speaking a word of Spanish, in the streets of Veracruz for some of my blood type which was unavailable in the whole state. They managed to find 6 pints of O negative blood as well as saving my life. There was a tsunami of love, generosity and support that came my way. And even though it was a traumatic terrible experience, at the same time, it sort of blew my heart open.

My life has been completely changed. I am a one-legged existentialist standup beat poet. Given that my name is Paradox and my life has been characterized by paradox. When I lost my leg, the worst thing that happened to me was also the best thing that ever happened to me...and it gets better all the time."

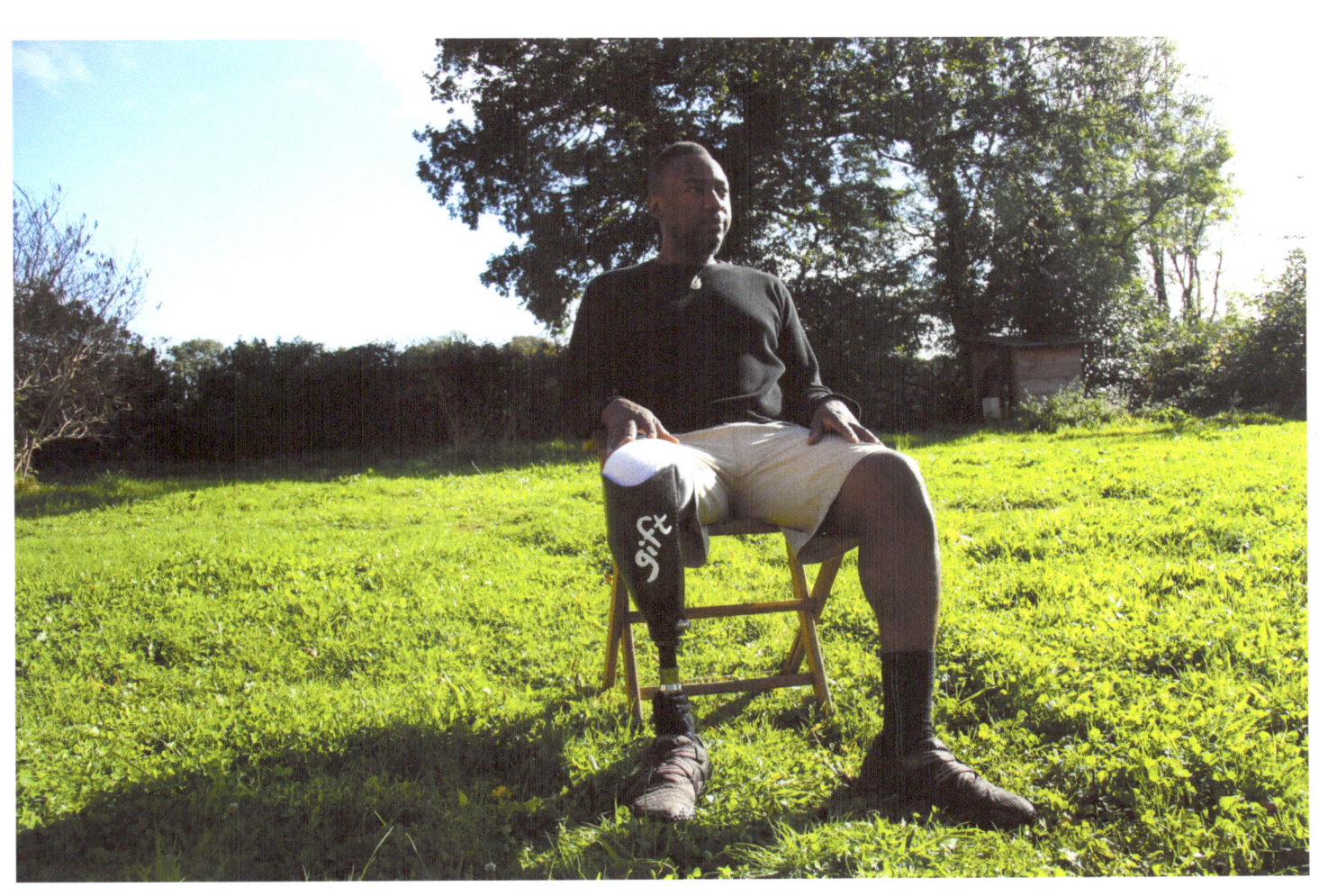

iRish

name: Inua
age: 26
born: Nigeria

Inua is friendly and full of vitality. He seems, at least to any nearby observer, to have an endless supply of energy. A sketchbook is his constant companion, in which he is consistently jotting down poems or sketching people and places around him.

This tall lean man grew up in Nigeria. His family fled persecution and was granted asylum in the United Kingdom when he was eleven. He has lived here ever since, with the exception of one year when he and his family lived in Dublin, Ireland. He was the only black child in the entire school and understood completely that this was a make or break time for him.

"I could fall into stereotypes or be myself in all my quirkiness. I wasn't going to manage to put on an act to be accepted, so I decided to be me." He excelled academically and was an easy organiser. At one point, a school activity required fundraising. He offered to take on the task himself and, in very short shrift, had raised the necessary funds for the school group. He was just being his own quirky self. "Not only did they accept me, they appreciated me for my unique qualities. This experience, this make or break point where I had to make a choice, helped me grow up. Ireland helped me grow up. And I found my place in the world."

Inua lives in London and works as a poet, a playwright, and a graphic designer. He also runs midnight walks. He offers these as a community building experience and a way to get to know the local environment from a completely fresh perspective.

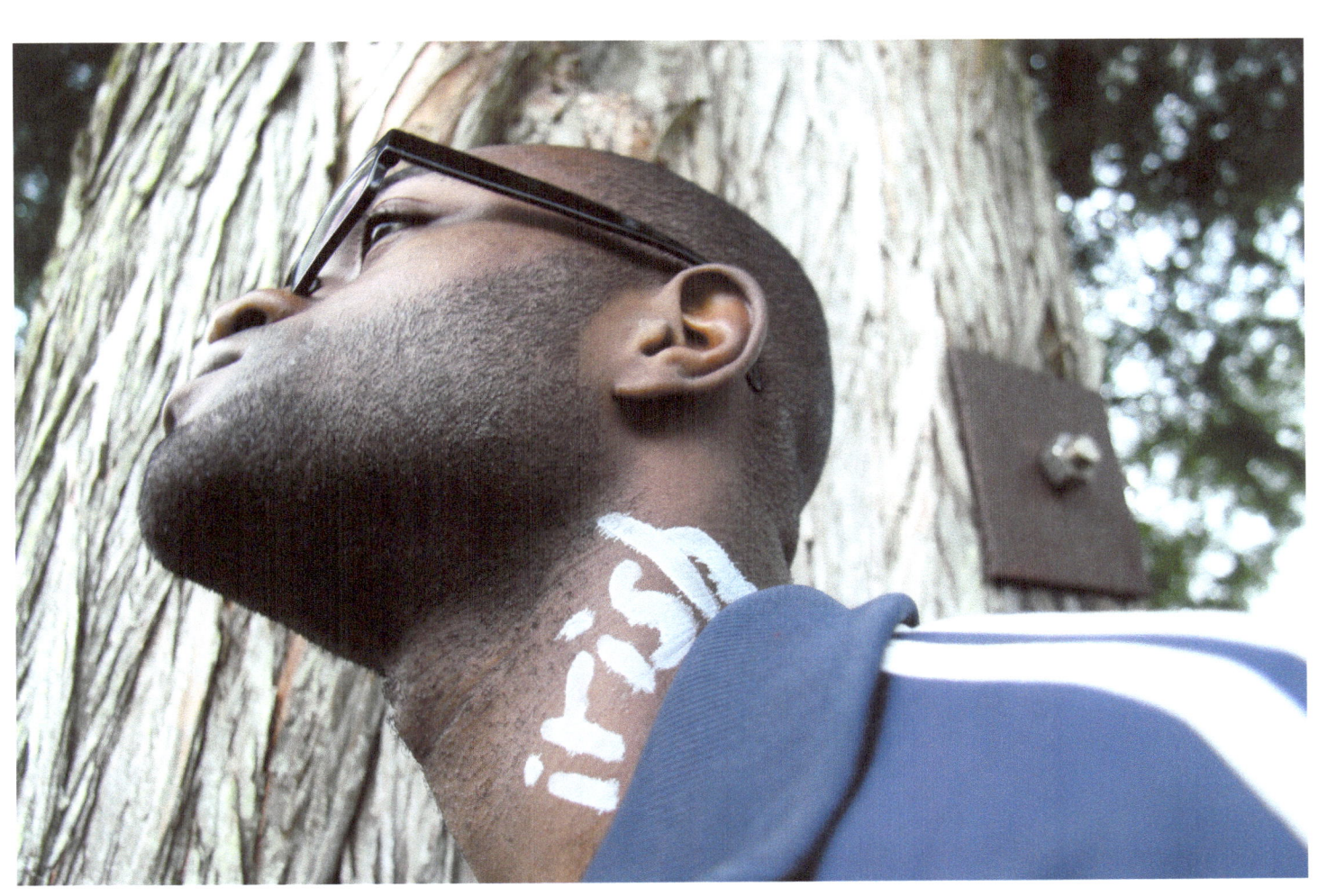

Ghetto Girl

name: Katheryn
age: 49
born: USA, Midwest

"If you saw me on the street you might think, 'white, middle class, healthy, middle-aged, confident, educated, creative type'. Most of these are true, at least in part. What you might not have guessed is that I grew up in the ghetto* with one of the highest crime and rape rates in the USA. I call it a war zone to help explain to the strictly gun controlled British where I now live. Death and crime were such a mundane part of life in Gary. When we left, it felt too taboo for me to share that I had grown up in this place to the point that eventually I simply didn't offer this information to anyone for decades. It was somehow too vulnerable and shameful and I would be vague when asked. It is only in more recent years when I am feeling more of my own depth of presence that I can embrace my history. And increasingly, I realize the tremendous gifts I have been given from these experiences.

As I have accepted and acknowledged my ghetto history, it has unfolded as a source of strength and resilience. And somehow, something hidden then revealed releases power, grace, and gratitude in me too."

*I went back to downtown Gary, Indiana for this photograph with my son as photographer and a bodyguard. We shot it in the exquisite downtown cathedral ruin. We had one of the most wonderful enlivening days ever.

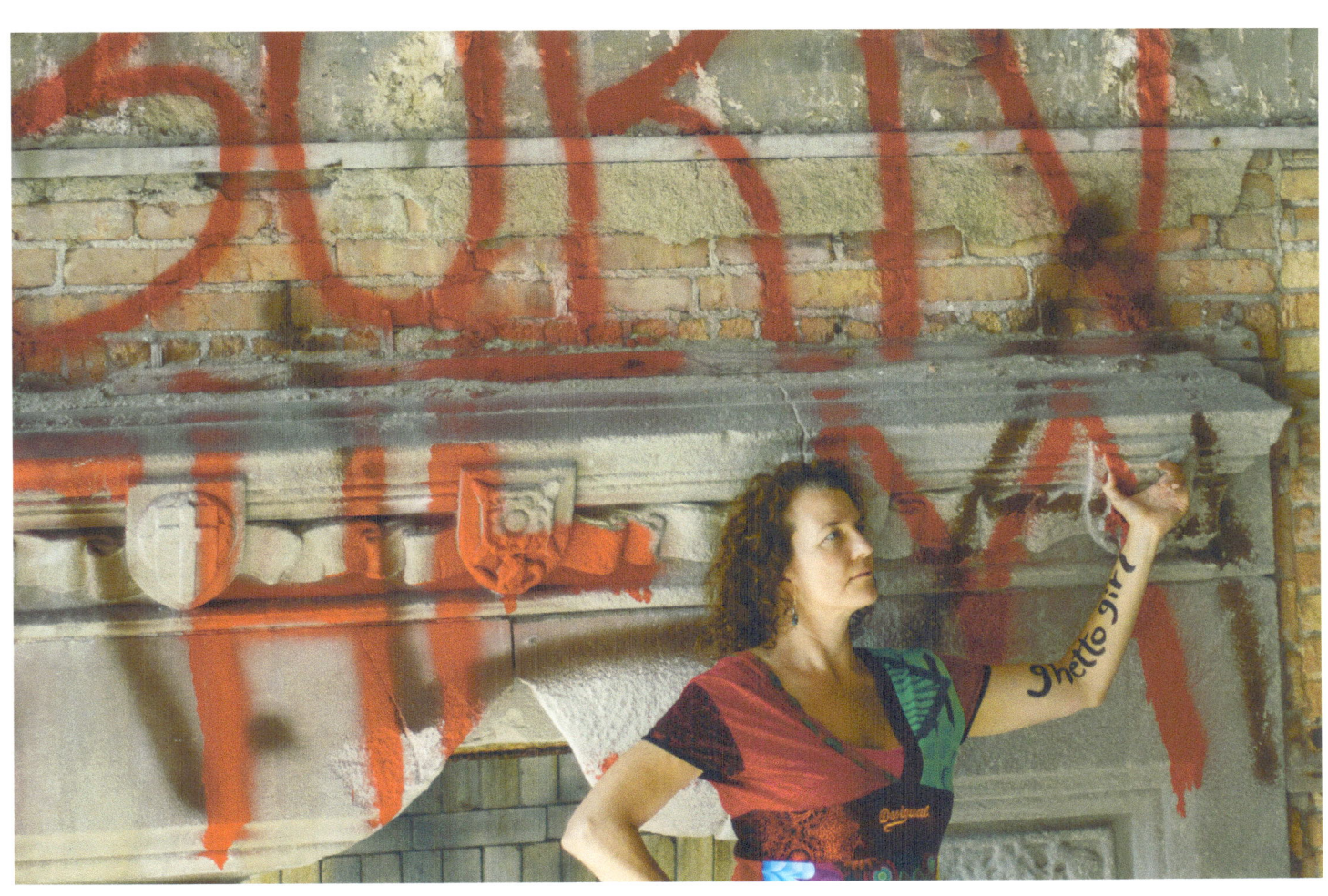

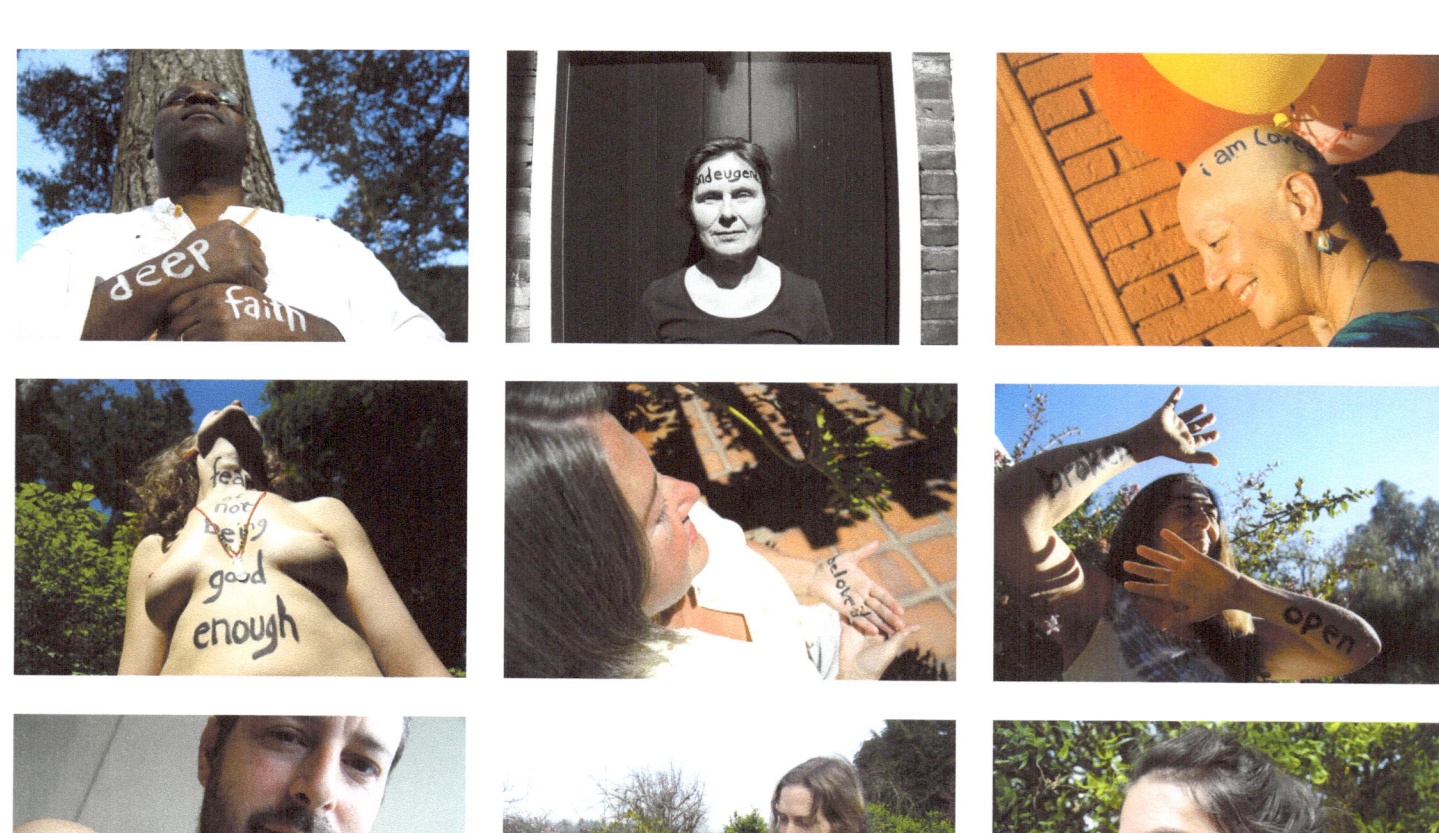

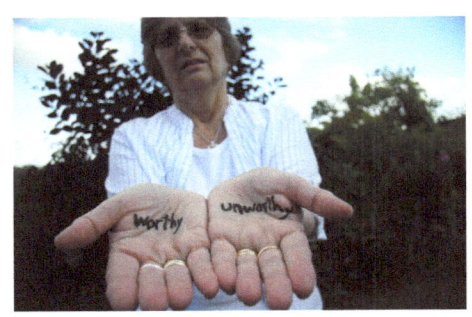 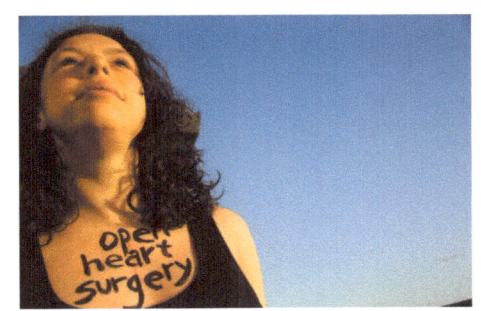 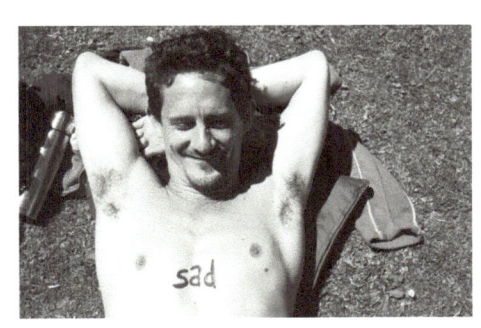

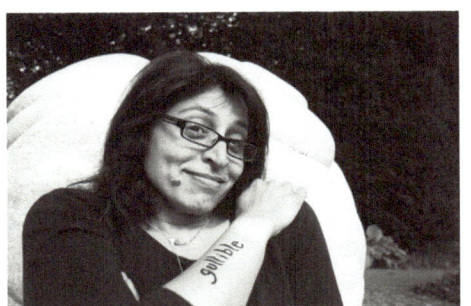 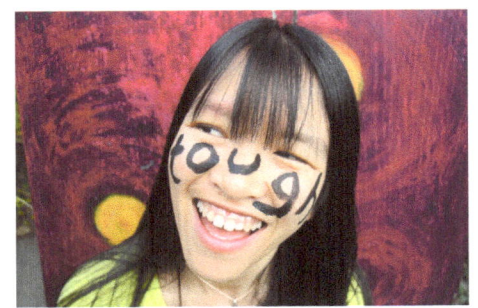 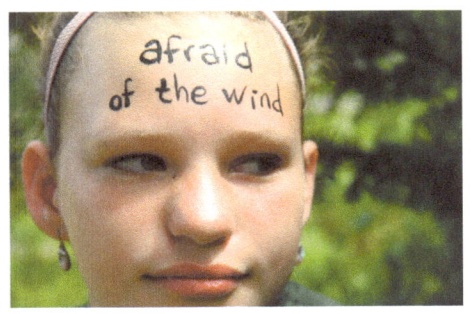

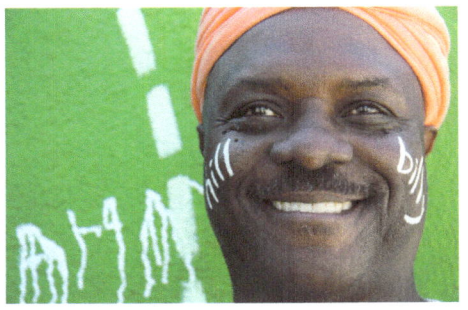 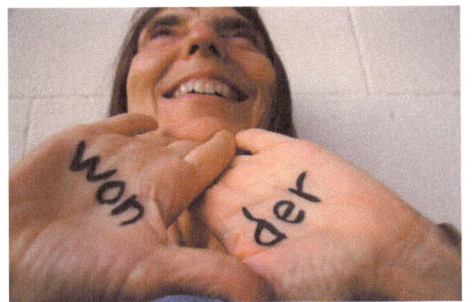 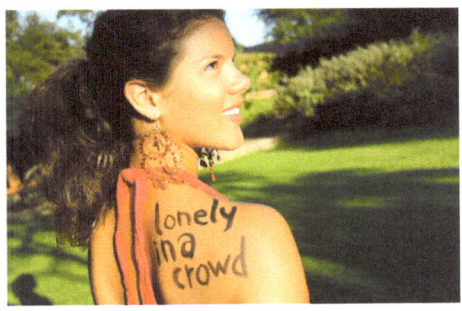

I'm just a sexual object

name: Dalale
age: 24
born: Morocco

Dalale is beautiful, intelligent and passionate about women and feminism. A Moroccan feminist in the face of these predominantly strict Muslim ways is quite something. And she spoke for many who could not.

This young woman's answer to the question, "what is true of you but not obvious to strangers?" for the project was clear. She wanted the no holds barred truth of her experience of this cultural context that she knows, suffers and also loves deep and true. "I'm just a sexual object", she writes ironically and elegantly in Moroccan Arabic down her arm.

We are in public. I know she risks more than any one so far for this photograph. She and I are frequently moved to tears in our interview. She is so courageous. She is also making a stand for healing this very wound in her culture and heart. Her daily life consists of 20 to 40 times a day, she says, being verbally, physically and sexually attacked or assaulted. Some subtle. Some blatant. But all of these experiences cumulatively affecting this woman's life, psyche and heart. She is also clear that by being a feminist film maker in a country where it is forbidden for women to do so many things is how she plans to change things for future generations at home.

Dalale is a beautiful bridge between worlds.

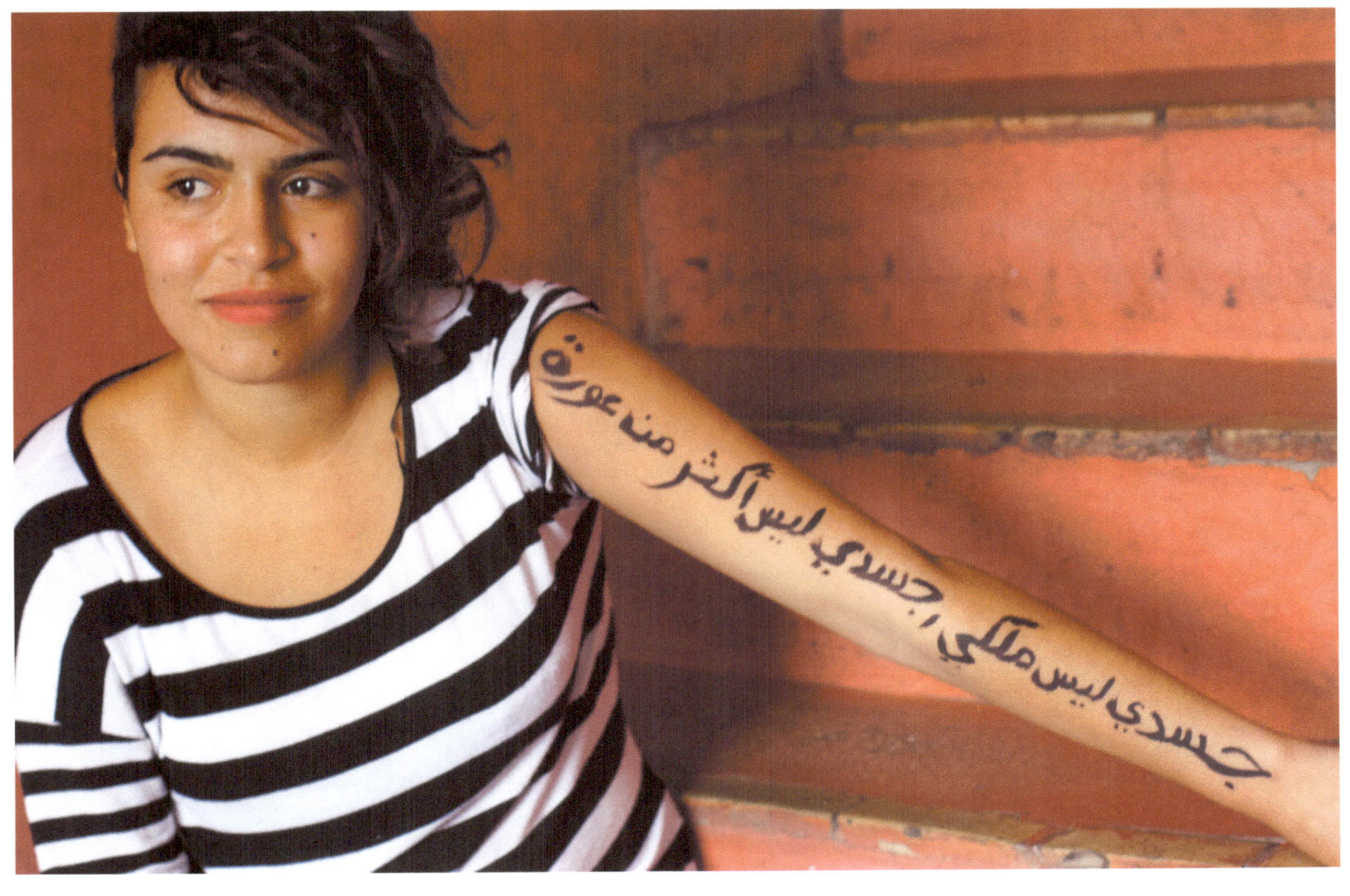

body conscious

name: Lee
age: 24
born: England

I had been sharing for months with my hairdresser, Lee, about the *In Your Own Skin* project. He was intrigued. I invited him to participate. He agreed and so the dance began of choosing a time for the portrait and of course what words he would allow me to paint in simple black onto his skin somewhere. He wanted to find just the right words. We discussed them at length as he cut my hair one day. Several times he thought he had arrived at the words he wanted to share. We explored several options on his short list and arrived at the best one. Then, just before we went to take the photograph, he changed his mind. "Body conscious," he blurted out. He and I both knew that this was more important for him to share than anything else.

Here was this young, fit, fine-looking man. People often told him how lucky he was to be so skinny and not have to worry about weight. The reality was that

Lee had struggled every day of his entire life. He often felt ashamed of his ribs poking through his abdomen and worried about how he would take care of his growing family as breadwinner. He needed to weigh enough to have a healthy lifestyle. He had a condition that actually kept him thin and which required constant vigilance. No one knew except his closest family and friends, and each time someone made a comment, he would be reminded of this illness and smile in silence.

When we were finished with the photographs, he said, "Wow! I see now. It's not the portrait that's the art actually. The real art is this conversation and the relief of sharing this uncomfortable secret. I feel lighter and more joyful and suddenly like it's a powerful thing to share with other young men who struggle with hidden illnesses and related weight issues."

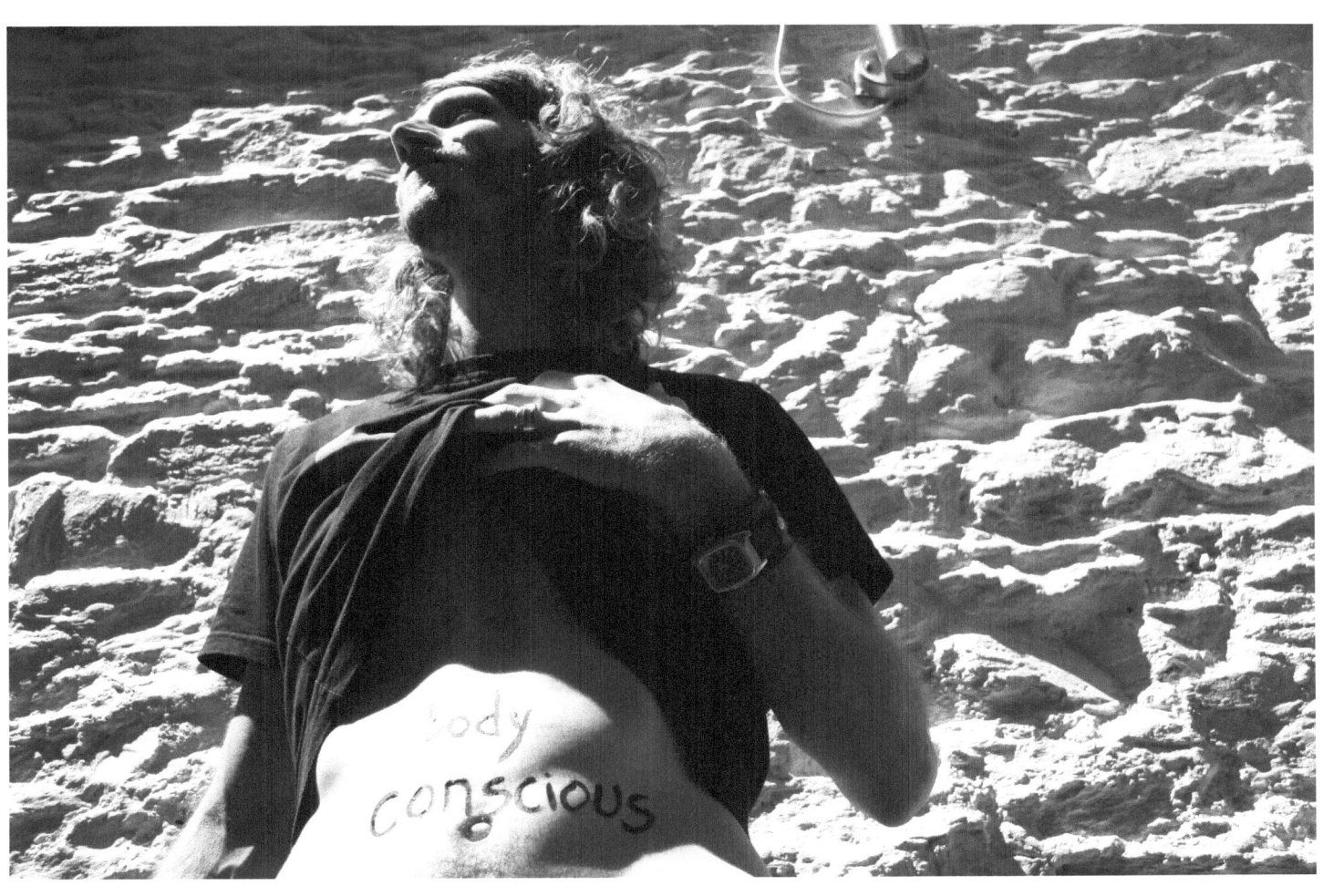

i miss my brother

name: Nicholas
age: 49
born: Belgium

Nicolas is from Brussels and plays guitar all over the
world for some of the finest musicians and performers.
When I asked him to share something true but not
obvious to strangers, he knew at once. "I miss my
brother." I have actually known Nicholas for decades
through his wife, but did not know this about him. His
vulnerability as he shared this grief that never quite
goes away feels like relief when made visible and
palpable. It is almost as if by sharing, he is supporting
not only himself but his family, his environment and
the collective unconscious. His access to this part of
himself seems all the more touching and inspiring. He
grants a generous permission to us all to take the time
it takes to experience our grief as it spirals through
him and us in waves.

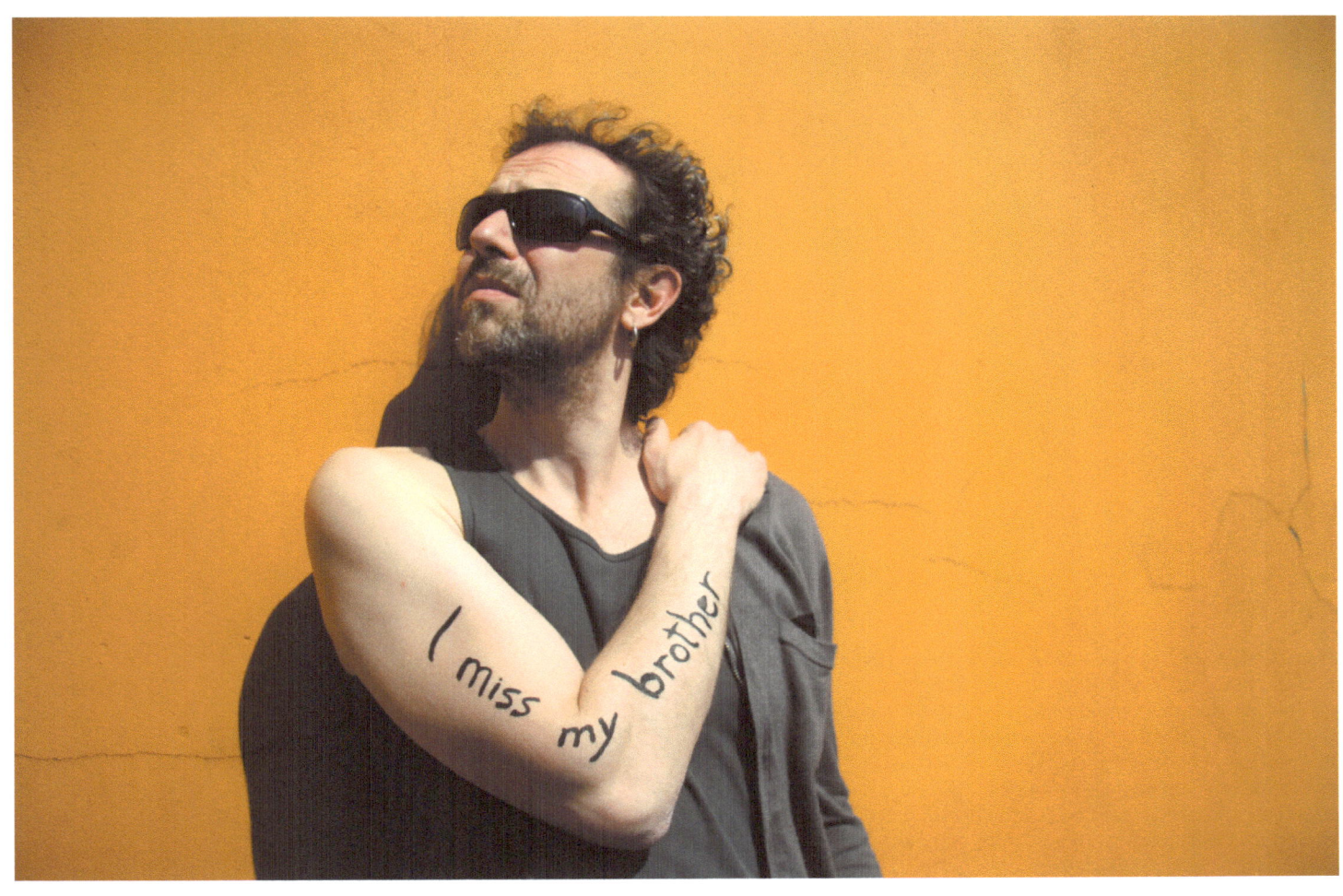

cReative

name: Samantha
age: 35
born: India

She is an hotelier at an exclusive hotel with a Michelin star restaurant attached. This beautiful being who creates home away from home for so many has not yet had many "officially" creative opportunities. And yet, she is just about to create the ultimate oeuvre - Life. She feels her creative expression is just about to be born too. She is learning to write poetry. How delicious to feel all that potential and vitality we all hold.

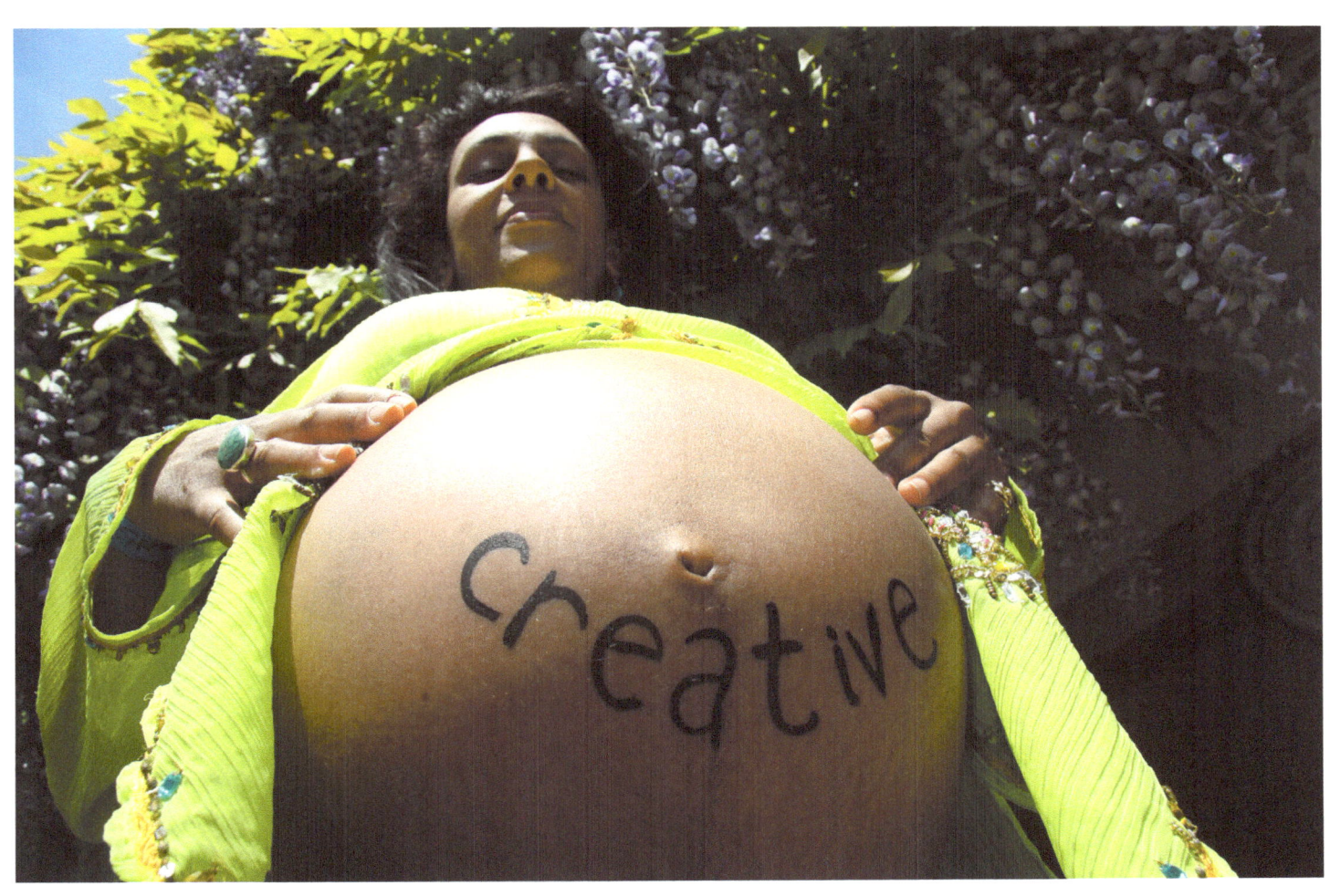

je n'oublie rien / I never forget

name: JK
age: 78
born: Belgian Congo

JK is the proud vibrant 78-year-old chief of a tribe
in what is now called The Democratic Republic of
Congo. He has had a varied and colorful life. He speaks
4 languages plus several local dialects. He chose to
share "je n'oublie rien," owning that he forgets neither
the kindnesses that have been bestowed upon him,
nor the ill. He is not easy to forget a grudge and knows
that this costs him, his family and his tribe. When his
daughter saw what words he chose, she smiled wryly
from ear to ear and said that was perfectly true.

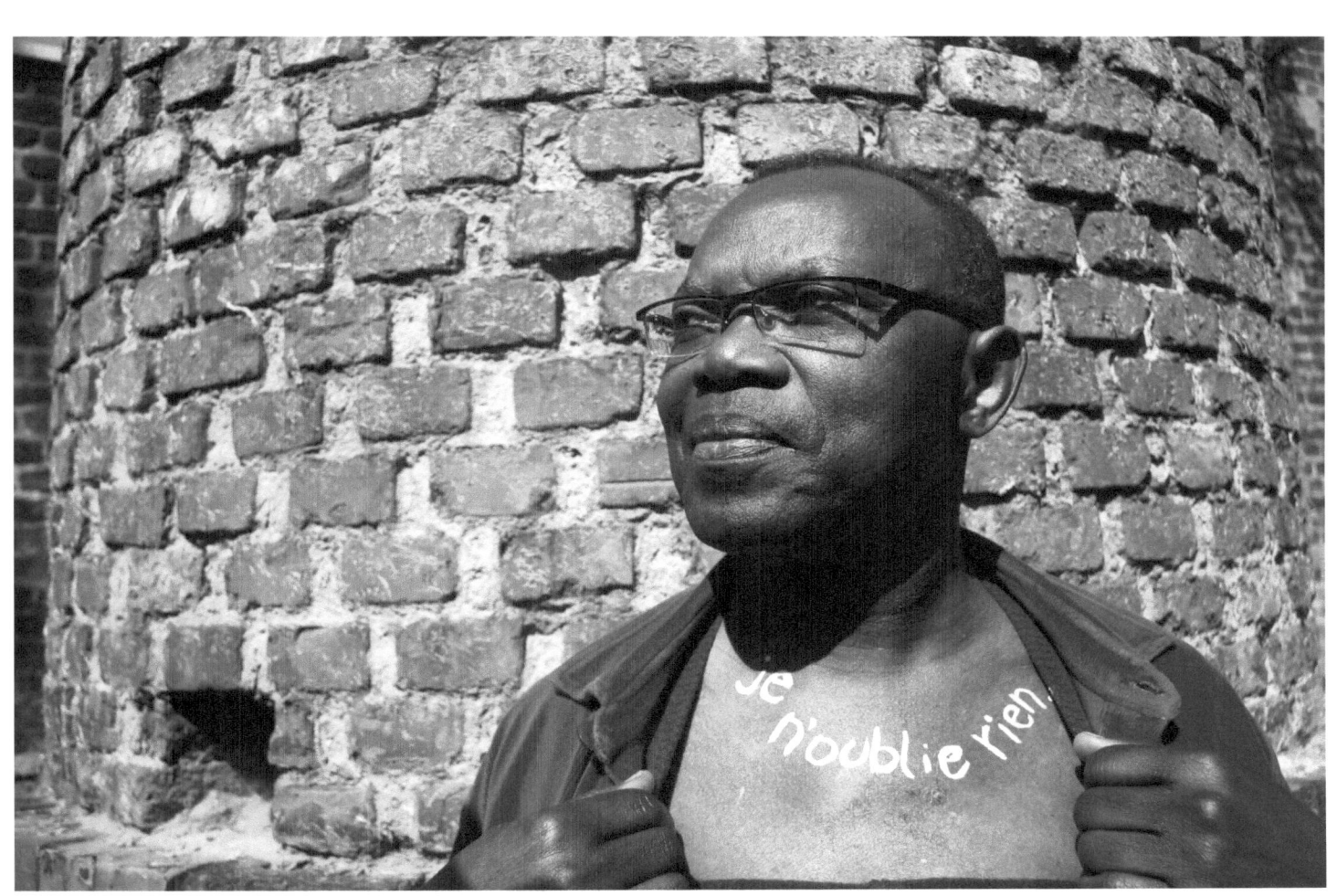

boites a secrets / confidant

name: Zohar
age: 13
born: Belgium

Zohar is a 13-year-old student. He is easy-going,
kind and intelligent. He is African, European, Jewish,
the son of down to earth performance artists, the
grandson of doting salt of the earth grandparents.
This boy looked deep to find his expression to share.
He realized, through the inquiry, that one of the
most powerful roles he plays in his tightly woven
community of friends is being the one they confide in
and trust. He is their confidant, their boites a secrets,
literally - box for secrets, where friends can lay down
their troubles and know they will be honored and held
safe.

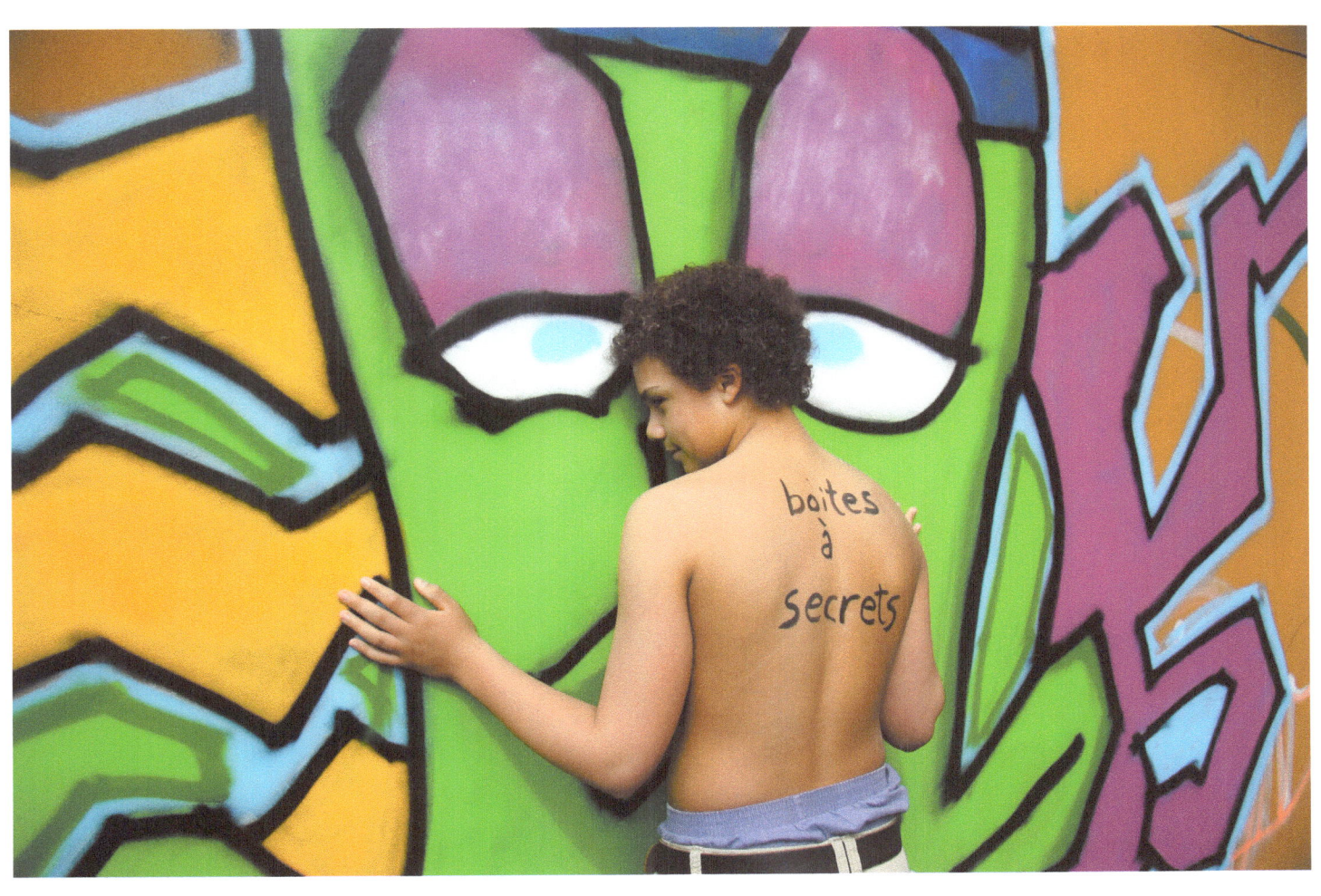

cocaine

name: Anonymous
age: 24
born: England

I love this portrait for many reasons, not least of which is the courage it took to allow it to be made. But, even more importantly, I enjoy how this embodies a phenomenon we all know in some way. People make a projection about what this young woman's story is. Very few could ever guess it. People also respond to this portrait with empathy. Even though they may have never used cocaine, they probably do know what it's like to be addicted to other drugs legal or illegal depending on the country they're living in, coffee, sugar, work, or...

This woman did use cocaine. She was in a relationship with someone who was into that, and she liked the way it made her feel beautiful in herself. She didn't like anything else about the drug. She only experienced it a few times, but it had a profound effect on her life. She's been trying to figure out a way to feel that beautiful ever since and comfortable in her skin without using substances. Who among us has never known some kind of deep longing for something else? Who among us doesn't want to feel beautiful and at ease?

"It was a beautiful experience being listened to and valued in my own skin."
-Anonymous, UK

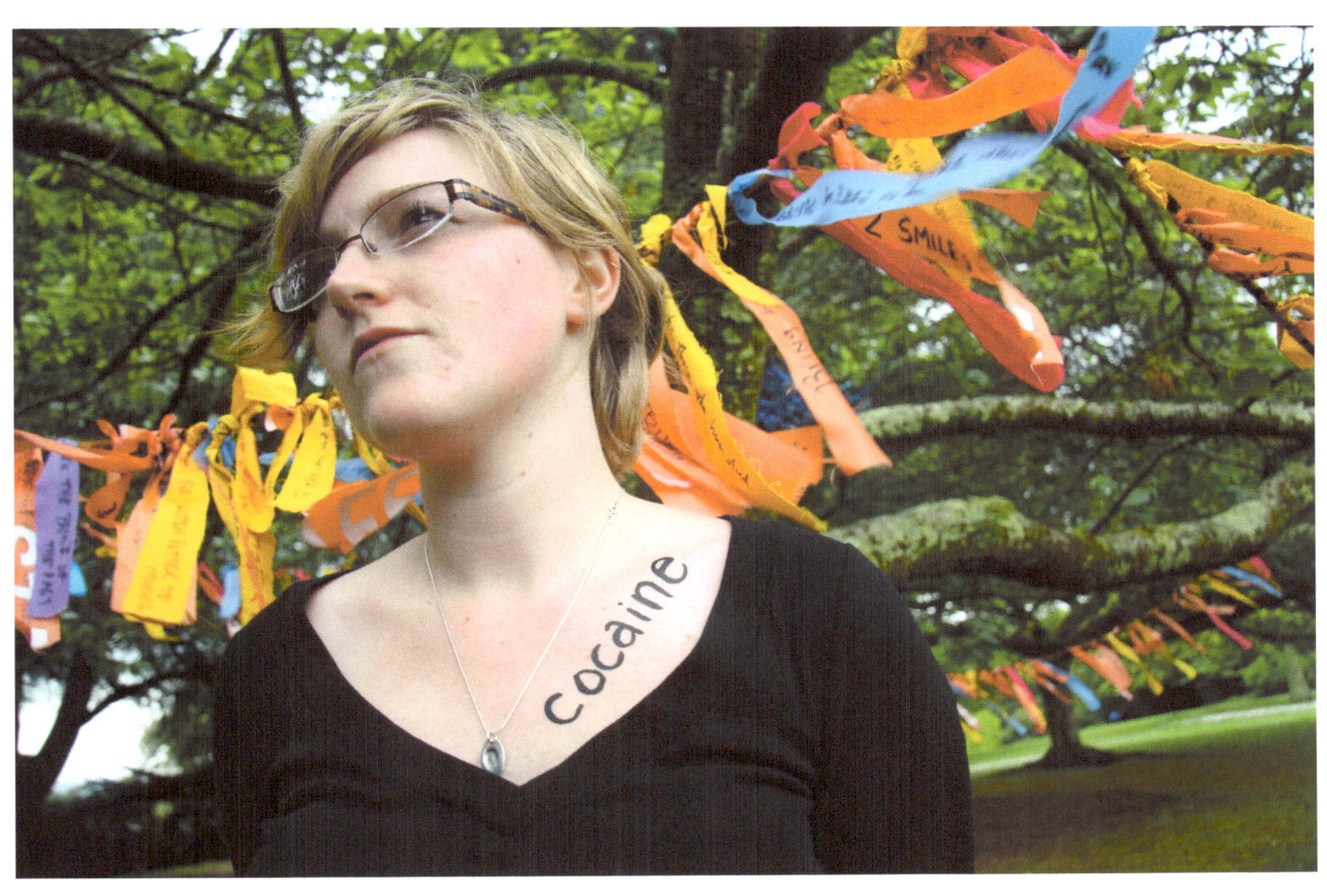

Raped from 6-9

HIV

i forgave my Rapists

name: Eric
age: 48
born: USA, Midwest

I met Eric by chance on my own personal peace pilgrimage to the spectacular fallen-beyond-any-hope-of-repair downtown Cathedral. Built in Gary's heyday by immigrant hands with steel mill riches. I invited Eric to sit for a portrait because I heard him singing gospel deliciously up to sky through gaping holes in the flying buttresses.

When I told him my question, he looked at me askance... and wondered if I were some kind of psychic. We laughed together and he then proceeded to list off some of the things you would be unlikely to guess about this handsome and charming man. The freedom he holds in himself is apparent and inspiring.

He even gifted us all with his exquisite rendition of the Our Father song standing where the altar would have once been. '...Give us this day our daily bread, and forgive us our trespasses, as we forgive those who trespass against us...'

There was not a dry eye by the time he was finished.

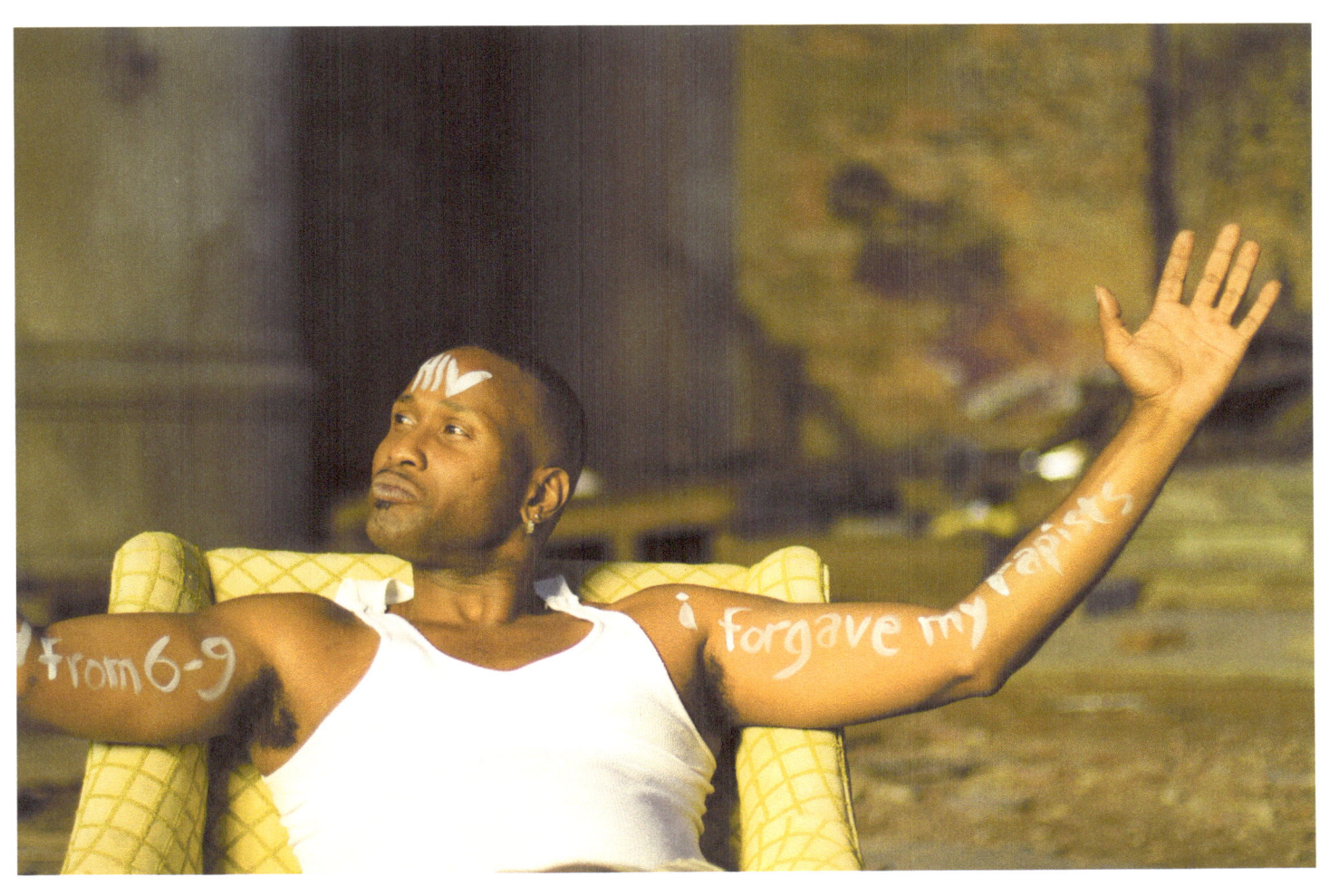

fierce

name: Matt
age: 48
born: UK

Matt's demeanor comes across as a bit vulnerable and very nice. He is also funny. That kind of intelligent dry wit that is so English and so wonderful. He says, for instance, with a very serious demeanor, that in addition to being a regular BBC Radio 4 performer, "his consuming interest in the core concerns of contemporary society has led him into many interesting shops." He looks younger than he is. He is kind and sweet. He could easily be projected upon as only this - Nice. As true as this is, so is the ferocity with which he passionately puts his pen to paper and creates the most extraordinary poems and prose. This fierceness is also evident in the way he parents, the way he loves, and the way he wields his writing talents for peace and parenting, tennis and truth, environment and eating, DIY and dreams.

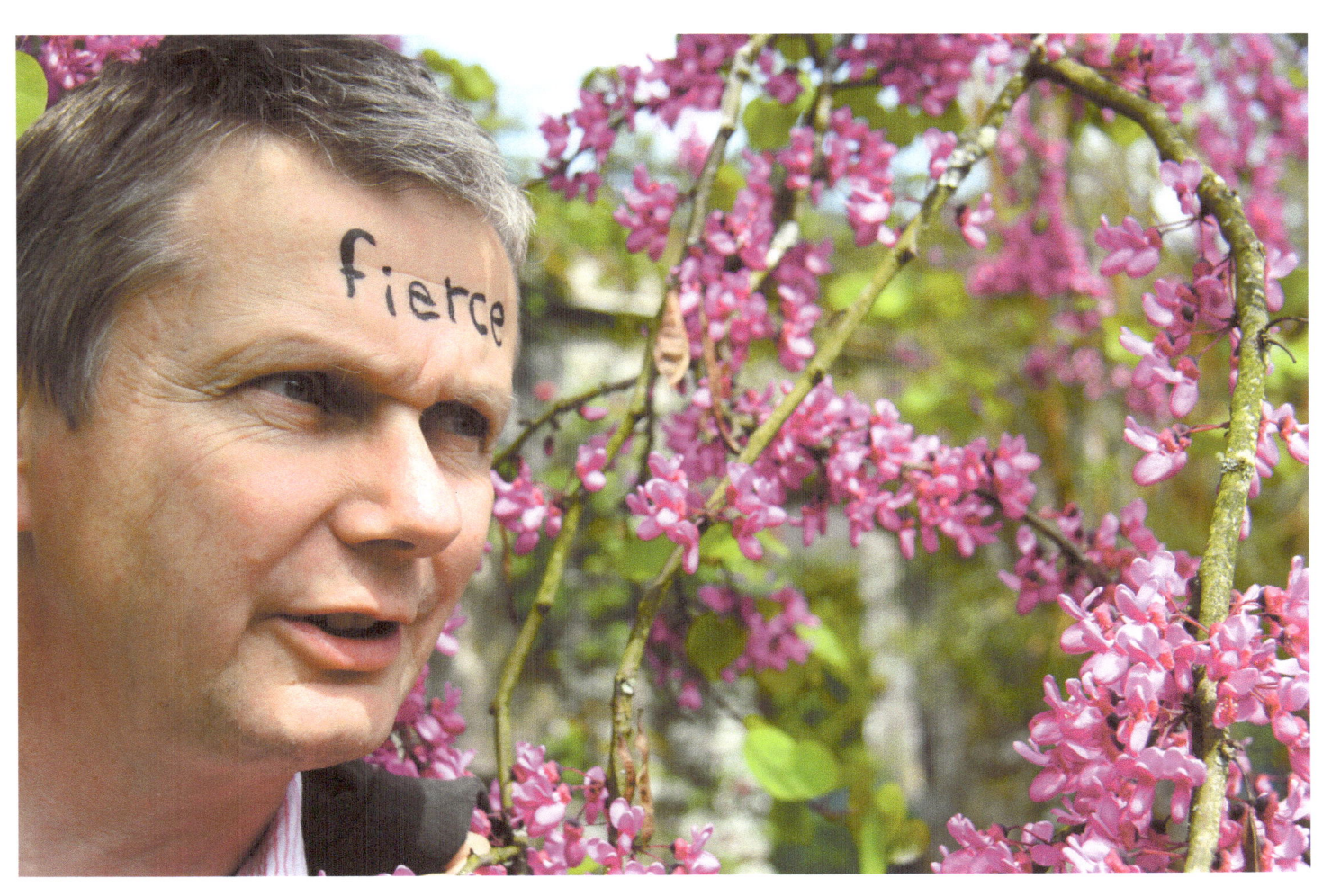

A taste of images from our *In Your Own Skin* Summer 2013 tour across the USA

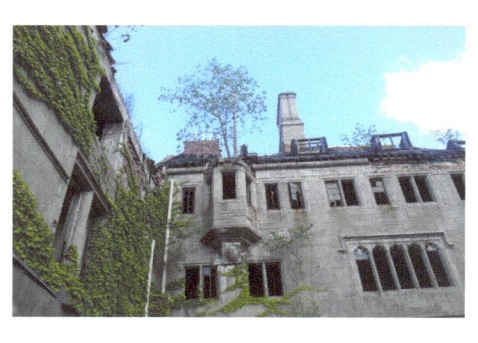
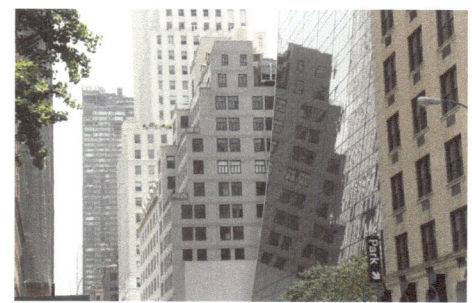
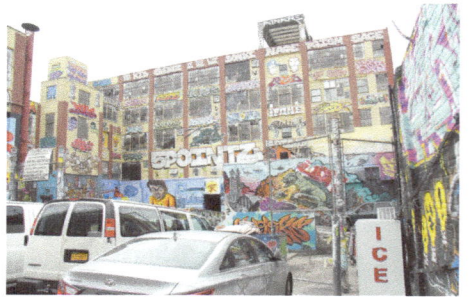
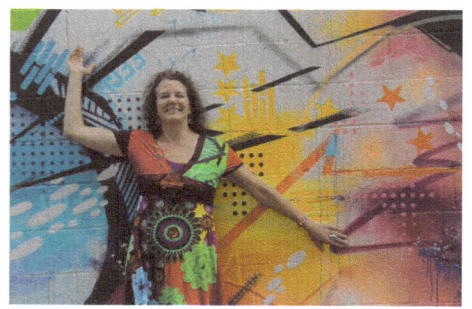
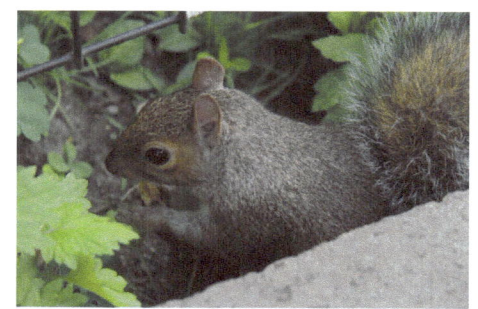
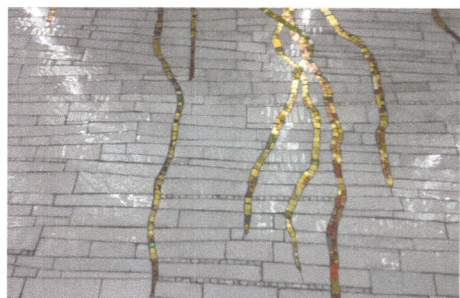
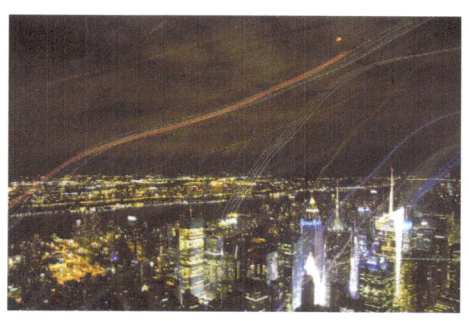
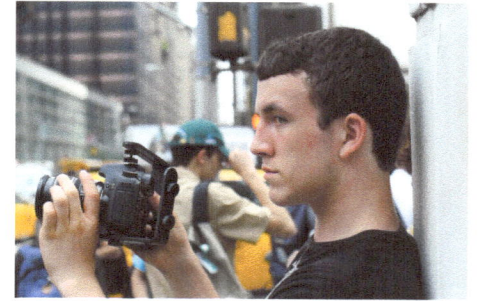
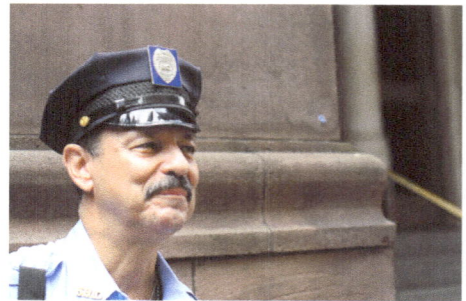

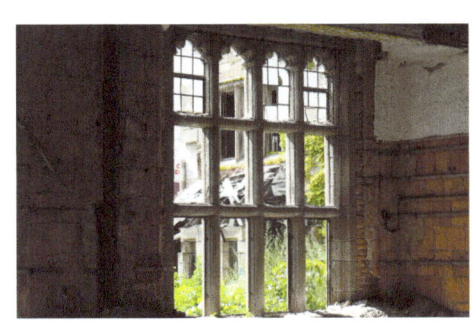 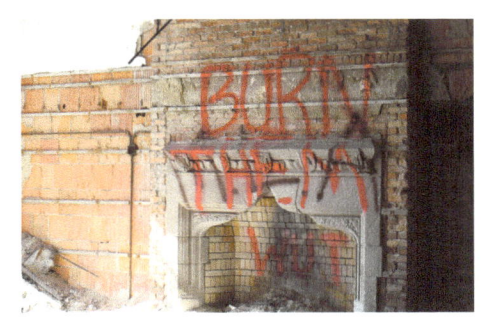 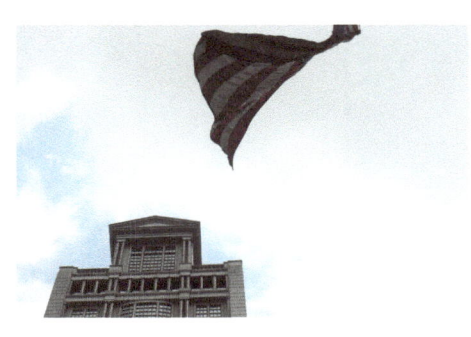

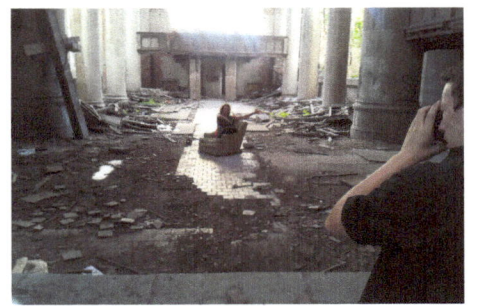 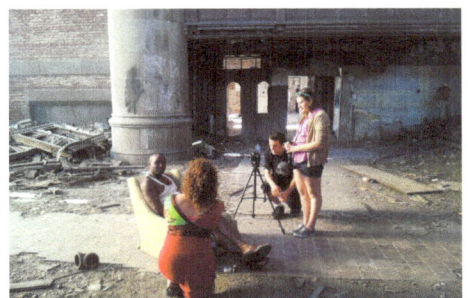 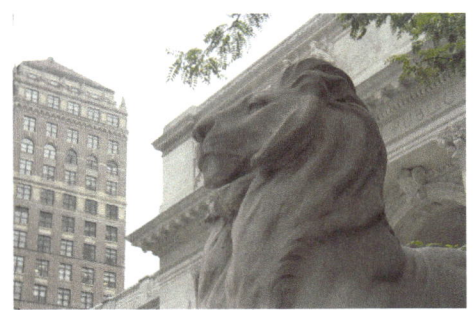

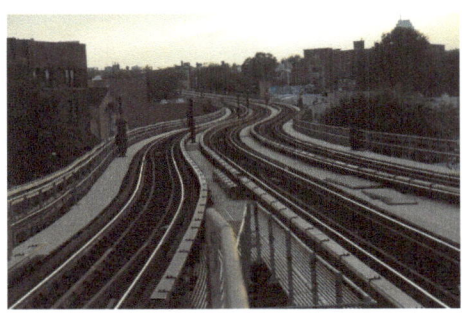 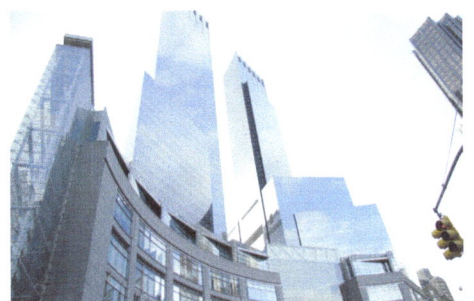 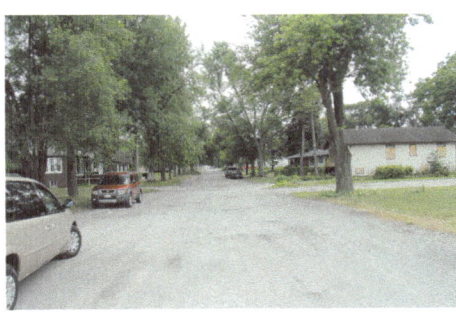

About Katheryn Trenshaw:

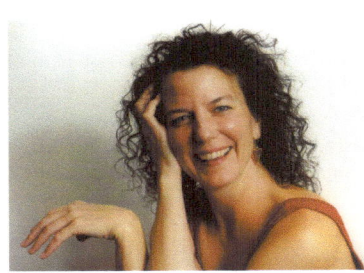

Katheryn Trenshaw is an American-born international artist, expressive arts teacher, and cultural creative living in England. Over the course of nearly thirty years, her work has been shown in galleries and educational venues in Europe, Asia, and North America. She has received numerous grants and commissions. Her photographs, sculptures, and paintings are prized in private collections, and have been shown in public buildings, including the United Nations.

She is the founder and creative director of *Passionate Presence Center for Creative Expression* (UK). The *Passionate Presence Center* is an international center through which Katheryn offers training and facilitation in movement, art, and personal development. She conducts educational events, workshops, multi-media projects, and does consulting for individuals, groups, and organizations in the United States, Europe, and around the world. Among many community activities, Katheryn also facilitates the Transition Town Totnes Arts Network.

Her exhibition, *Breaking the Silence*, a project for and about survivors of child sexual abuse, consisting of one hundred sculpted masks and multi-media elements, had a dramatic impact on both the media and the public in the early '90's and for the next fifteen years that it toured throughout the United States and Europe.

Currently, she lives in Totnes,Devon, England, one of the "the world's Top 10 Funkiest towns". There, overlooking Dartmoor National Park, she has a small organic orchard, four chickens, two cats, and a home and studio decorated in bright saturated colors like her paintings.

Thank you

Words cannot even begin to thank the thousands who have sown the seeds for this project. Here is but a small woefully incomplete and inadequate list of those who I wish to thank:

All those who have agreed to be photographed, painted and interviewed. I have cried and laughed and been moved to my core in the mysterious way that this process brings. I am very grateful to you and your gifts will keep on giving.

Cameramen, Editors, Volunteers, Administrative helpers and advisors. Your help past, present and future is invaluable.

My friends and hosts, old, new and future, who have been steadfast around the globe in support of the cause… Thank you for your generosity, patience and hospitality. We have experienced such an outpouring of kindness as we have toured.

The wonderful journalists who have so kindly believed in the project and shared it in powerful far reaching ways.

And to my many teachers over the decades, especially Adam, Marcy, Stan, Steph and Gary. And my parents who taught me about peace and reconciliation in a war zone long before Desmond and Nelson. You are an inspiration in so many ways for this very project. Without your openness to marvellous errors, wanderlust and generous madly creative hearts this *In Your Own Skin* Project would not exist.

And so many more…

But above all, my warm love goes to the bright creative spark, my son Orion, who has patiently and lovingly volunteered or "been" volunteered and traipsed around the globe for the cause with camera and recording equipment. You rock. May you always live lovingly and delightfully in your own skin, exactly as you are.

And thank you in advance for your loving support to make this project a reality.

How to become a part of the *In Your Own Skin* Project? Join us.

Thank you in advance for taking the time to support and bring to full fruition this antidote to human separation. With your support, the *In Your Own Skin* Multi-media Community Arts Project will be birthed as a fully formed entity. This small book gives a glimpse into what will be a complete multi-platform project: a **full**-length book featuring 100 *In Your Own Skin* portraits selected from among the hundreds of people photographed around the globe, a touring art exhibit with 2 meter^2 banners of portraits, a feature documentary and as workshops.

The *In Your Own Skin* Project was designed to serve our growing need as a culture to embrace the hidden truths that will ultimately set us free. Please take a moment to go to **www.inyourownskin.org** and become a part of this community.

Here you can join the *In Your Own Skin* Project and contribute in many ways by sharing links on all of your social media sites as well as financially via our crowdsourcing campaign. You can organize an *In You Own Skin* workshop or film screening in your community. And, you can also join the *In Your Own Skin* Project Facebook page, subscribe free to our YouTube channel, Newsletter and Blogs.

"We are made mostly of water...
and the rest is Stardust"

- Neil deGrasse Tyson

www.inyourownskin.org

First published in the UK by Passionate Presence Press 2014
© 2014 Katheryn Trenshaw
photographs copyright © 2014 by Katheryn M Trenshaw
photograph page 7 © 2014 Orion Trenshaw-Leggett
Text copyright © 2014 by Katheryn M Trenshaw
Printed in paperback 2014
First edition

Passionate Presence Press
Passionate Presence Center for Creative Expression
6 Broomborough Drive
Totnes
Devon
TQ9 5LT
UK
phone: +44 (0) 1803 863552
skype: katheryntrenshaw
facebook: inyourownskinproject
email: post@ktrenshaw.com
web: www.passionatepresence.org

A catalogue record for this book is available from the British Library

ISBN 978-0-9905420-0-1